Introduction

I began to write some poems in September 1987. At that time we moved house to Annvale just outside Keady. The Glen, the river Callan and the trees seemed to conspire together to make poetic thoughts well up. I wrote some poems and stories for Síol Le Gaoithe our local Comhaltas branch magazine with the encouragement of musical and set dancing friends. I'd like to thank these friends for their friendship and encouragement through the years. Some of the original poems have since been reprinted in books and papers with some favourable reactions. Here I have tried to gather some old favourites and some newer poems into a more balanced collection. My original thrust in writing was to try and preserve some of the thoughts and memories of childhood and of life in general. The joy of a simple moment, the challenges of life, the golden moments of love, the sadness of death, and other time stopping moments which happen to everyone but seem to pass somehow unrecorded. Seamus Heaney said a poem is "a photograph of a memory" and that's what I have tried to achieve. Not all of the poems are perfect but if there is one that evokes a memory in you or touches a common thread then I have done my job. Where there are Irish words in the text I have used them as the most appropriate words to capture the spirit of what I mean, the notes section contains explanations for these words. I hope you enjoy them.

Damien Mallon

Contents

READING THE TREES	7
THE UMBRELLA MAN	8
ON YOU BEING THERE AND ME BEING HERE	9
KEADY'S WATER WHEEL	10
EMPTY ENVELOPES AND RED EYES	11
THE AUCTIONEERS FOUNTAIN PEN	12
HEDGEROW SCHOOL	13
HALF OF AN OLD CINEMA TICKET	14
MOONWORDS	15
WINTERBOURNE	16
THE NEW LOLLYPOP MAN	17
THE HATCHERY	18
BALLYCASTLE DASH	19
AMERICAN WAKE	20
A SOLITARY BUSH	21
WILD MUSHROOMS	22
FORGETFULLNESS	23
SATURDAY NIGHT	24
THE BLACKTHORN STICK	25
STARS	26
A SPELL FOR YOU	27
SWANS DOWN	28
SHOES	29
RAIN TOMORROW	30

FINIAN	*31*
AWAITING AN OLD FRIEND	*32*
ASHLING AGAIN	*33*
KEADY GRAVEYARD SUNDAY	*34*
ONE SWALLOW	*35*
FIVE FOXGLOVES	*36*
AUDIE MURPHYS MEN	*37*
THE MORRIGAN IN WINTER	*38*
CAROLINES MORNING	*39*
THE AUCTION	*40*
THE CLOCK	*41*
THISTLEDOWN THOUGHTS	*42*
THE NO DIVORCE COURT	*43*
ABOVE THE SOUNDS OF WATER	*44*
RAYMOND	*45*
THE MAN IN THE MOON	*46*
THE COCKFIGHT	*47*
CEAPING A HEIFER	*48*
THE RAINDANCER	*49*
JOURNEY	*50*
AFTER THE SNOW	*51*
THROUGH THE MILL	*52*
THE PATH	*53*
SKIMMING STONES ON THE CALLAN	*54*
A PUB UNDER THE TREES	*55*
IF ONLY A LITTLE	*56*

READING THE TREES.

For Tony Crozier.

You couldn't know but now
You are reading the trees,
The ones from Carnagh woods
They were felled late last autumn,
That whole green hillside's now a-stubble
Grabbed up in twig-like bundles
To be mulched into paper.
But I remember when summer rainbows
Foretold of westerly rain showers in arches
Over your emerald peaked canopy
I sheltered under this very one,
Touched the bluebell's bells
Watched an ant climb a trumpet mushroom.
I kissed a girl against that one,
She wore a summer cotton print dress
I picked the bark-moss off her back
As we walked on together through the trees.
In the autumn ferns under those two
Planted too closely together,
A wounded cock pheasant sheltered
'Till a busy spaniel took him to hand.
In here the soldiers sheltered
Men with woolly faces conspired
Wood pigeons flighted to dusky roosts
And the big tawny owl hoot-hooted.
The trees would rather we remembered them alive
In the musty smell of forest floor
In the stickiness of their amber sap
In these few lines written on their skin.

THE UMBRELLA MAN.

When our worlds were blown inside out

You came quietly to fix things

With your gentle way and swarthy skin.

Sitting cross-legged on the step

An Irish Gandhi in an old navy suit,

We small students gathered around you.

Braces of broken heroncrans your offerings

These black storm-blasted things

Twisted like silhouetted spiders webs,

You recreate their domes by magic

Teaching them to fly again

With spines from your steel hedgehog

And steady twitching pulls of your hands,

Each one opened with a final flurry

Satisfied something useless has been made useful.

After tea and a tanner you'll go

Gaily rattling like a broken accordion

Off down Davis Street to mend the town.

Leaving an opened arch above each of us

The world of the impossible made possible

And the knowledge of things learnt without words.

On you being there and me being here.

I saw you at your aunt's funeral on Tuesday
A twist of your hair was gently flapping
Out of your favourite sycamore leaf scarf
During that one final sorrowful decade.

Your long fingers picked the red apple
As I reached for the green in the market
A sideways glance was enough for me
Your blue blue eyes still sparkle.

Your ankles in brown punched shoes crossed
On the Keady bus gave me such a thrill
Though you know I could show no reaction
A little heart is noted by the whist players.

The queue for the Geography Form Teacher
Has been our only few words and smiles
Parents and teachers all around us
An island of innocence, you went before me.

No need I know, you think, for me to write this
For you know and I know, that's enough,
And I'm not sure what we can ever do
About you being there and me being here.

Keady's Water Wheel.

Happy again to see you turning
With the clearest waters churning
In your sluices fresh from Clea.

Toss it high it arches downwards
Send it ever rain bowing onwards
Silver circles in the spray.

Joyous movement without effort
Feels as good as you remember
In your creeks you seem to say.

Not to beetle now nor mill
The giant turbine blade is still
Redundant relic of a bye-gone day.

For you've a modern job to do
Stop a bus of Yanks or two
Keep them here along their way.

Keady Graveyard Sunday.

You always met me near the angel
Down by the concrete path.
We'd replay all the matches
And a have a real good laugh.
There'd be talk about dogs
And where the pheasants lie.
Then we'd cup our hands in prayer
And try hard not to smile.
When they read the list of the departed
You always looked at me.
As we heard the names of those we knew
And stood there solemnly.
I hope you're near the angel
For you're not here this year.
But still my eyes went round the crowd
For the one that I'd held dear,
And only then I missed you
And I hurt for your "bit of crack"
But only when they read your name
I knew you'd not be back.

Empty Envelopes and Red Eyes.

Sitting here
With empty envelopes
And red eyes.
Every plate in the house
Has been washed, twice.
In our Sunday best
Amid a kindly chatter.

It's time for the unusual visitors
To leave now.
Realising in knowing
Fraternal glances and biting smiles,
Brave faces all to the fore.

"Goodbye, see you soon, in better times..."
Firmly hands are shaken,
Shoulders reassuringly slapped.
We return again
To the quietened house.

The Auctioneer's Fountain Pen.

Your power was in that gold and green fountain pen

Its senatorial arrow in a light grasp modern fasces

Directing legions to war, gold treasure vaults to be opened,

Signing receipts for conacre of twenty guineas with 2½% fees,

Opening its twin-sworded nib into precise and practised swirls.

Emptied of its trustworthy black life it was opened in private

Its silver biceps bending to gurgle in a froth of new importantness.

Rolled between extended fingers it clacked on your wedding ring

Or clasped gently between the lips a pensive prop cigar to muse

Glimpsing back into the darkness of smuggling and favours bought.

Lord of the cattle men, you don't need your ash plant now

When just a note will tumble the piers of your enemies

And a tap of your pen will knock a regarded lot to a friend.

HEDGEROW SCHOOL.

I spoke to the wren and she said "No"
Mankind alone won't teach you
All things, she said, you need to grow.

Take your questions to the trees
Follow the hedgehog all by night
And for directions ask the bees.

Sleep where only wild flowers show,
Turn your mind to the bluebell bank,
And grip like the dipper in the flow.

Enjoy the slow progress of the snail,
But listen in darkness like the bat
The fluttering moth carries a tale.

Taste the sweetness of dark berry fruits
Dock takes the sting from young nettle shoots
And remember the cure in wild garlic root.

Make all your plans by the spider's web
Listen at dawn to what each bird says
And don't move on till the haws go red.

Half an Old Cinem a Ticket.

It moves from old pockets into new

My treasured half a memory of you,

Once we carbon-hazed and wide-eyed

Were for a few hours side by side.

I close my eyes projected in my mind

The scene when your hand envelops mine

Pressed together in the darkness there

both players of a dream we shared.

Alone in the dark now never forget

You were half of an old cinema ticket.

MOONWORDS

"A circle round the moon – a storm is coming soon"
Old Irish Proverb

I adored the way you spoke to me in whispers
And wanted the sound never to stop
Never for there to be silence between us
And your words hung in the light
Moving slowly silverly towards me,
You wanting no one else to hear
Not even the moon to hear
Your moonwords to me.
Lying there naked in its corpse-white light
The sheets ruffled in cirrus circles
Out of the bed, the pillows splayed.
If will power alone could stop time
We would still be there frozen
Moonbeamed, mid-word, mid-joy,
A Pompeian couple in a dust of white love-ash.
But I knew the sky's first red star would soon
Call the golden strands of the day,
That moonwords alone could not hold
The coming storm for us.

Winterbourne.

I hear cascading voices calling

In your carried news of Winter,

Hopelessly in recurring echoes

Whispered by lovers in June,

"Always, I will love you,"

"I will, always, love you,"

"I will love you, always,"

passing in its final refrain

through un-formed doorways

magically opened by falling ash keys

and washed in your gushes,

the nettle seems finally

to have lost its sting.

The New Lollypop Man.

Your black boots are out forever

Of guttery trenches

And shining like the wet asphalt road,

Where you, made brawny

By forty years on the long tail

Too powerfully stand.

Now, with shovel up-turned

In two hours each day,

You'll learn gentleness again,

Taking small white hands

Into that sandpaper fist,

So carefully, like banties eggs,

From nest to kerbside nest.

Out from under the gangers glare,

Now, your only care,

Is from here to there.

The Hatchery.

For Oliver

The path was barred by padlocks

On gates and doors, windows built up

It was a secret secret place in the shade

Maybe where gold or silver was vaulted

Away from the untrusted and prying eyes

And when the last big brass padlocks fell open

It was more than wonderful to young wide eyes.

Water gurgled to and through all the tanks

And hundreds and thousands of fry

Fanned through our opened fingers

With each oxygen rich boil of the cool clear water

Three big tanks had brown trout fry

With their red dots along the lateral line

The small tank had recently hatched

Salmon eggs with gold albumen sacks

A one month ball and chain for the alevin.

The salmon parr had fingerprints on their flanks

A sign from the hand of god they were to be kings

A mesh box of salmon's eggs was being riddled in the current

A new court of leaping princes to tail dance at the weir

These were the eggs of the salmon of knowledge

I held up a double-handful into the sunlight that beamed

From the open door lighting my face in the reflected gold

The echoing water dripped from catacombed ceilings

The fry circled tiny in thousand schools around me

And a millennium of untold stories flooded my mind.

BALLYCASTLE DASH.

Tullyherim, Derrynoose.

That old cottage on the height is derelict

Its roof collapsed and door frames rotted

Even the jamb wall windowpane is broken

But on the walls the Ballycastle dash lustre's,

Sea snails, periwinkles, razorshells, mussels,

Spirals, black-blue polished and mother of pearl insides,

Wave-washed breaker-boiled round pebbles

Walked on by barefoot strand strollers,

Broken blue medicine hall glass here and there

Revives the deep azure memories of the shells

Mirror smithereens reflect the sunbeams in silver

Holding the whole structure on a spidersweb of light.

The round white granite stones of Newgrange's walls

Came from Wexford's foreshores by coracle,

So you came too, by ass and cart from Omeath

And on by Camlough and Slieve Gullion.

American Wake.

On these bales of hay
I ended my stay.
With pot-oven stew
And home grain brew.

With song and laugh
On these bags of chaff,
Musicians played
To the end of my day.

Then Séan O'Neill
Swung us both in a reel,
'Til we broke down in tears
Rembering life's lost young years.

Mary-Rose couldn't look
But she kissed me so deep,
Through her salty tears
I tasted goodbye, Oh my dear!

The old people stayed a while
To pray on their goodbyes,
Touching my hair like a child
And keening with tears and sighs.

So say a sad goodbye to Érin
Among these bags of grain,
I'm crying now, for crying's sake
A lonely corpse at his American wake.

A Solitary Bush.

I can't explain how attractive
A solitary bush is at twilight
In the middle of a green field.

Youthfully not quite yet a tree
Shoot-green young saplight leaves
Grabbing the fading light in twigfuls.

Its frozen top stooped over permanently
From the west wind pushing at its back
Giving it seemed direction and movement.

Are you tripping back from the well?
With full buckets tippling at your skirts
Checking stock with a weathered eye
In hardly turns of your unkempt head.

Or you're spying on your neighbours
Caught shamelessly now in the open
A shaking branch-hump on your back
Eyes averted, you can't even look at us;

Away, on you go then, never moving.

Wild Mushrooms.

For John Sheridan

The dogs had gone in way ahead of us
We hung back waiting for the shot,
Then pushing on through the hedge
Thorns scratching on wax coats and gun-metal
We saw them in dappled morning sunlight
A swathe of white helmets lining the hedgerow.

Here in this October hollow
Field mushrooms had flushed
Little groups of four or five
Hats tilted together in apparent conversation
Like pilgrims or mart men smoking in spore circles
Some with heads tilted back in laughter.

"Here's the breakfast" said John
And picking the longest rush stalks
He began pulling the mushrooms
Threading each one with a practiced nimbleness
Onto the rushes needlepoint tops.

In a few minutes we were bandoleered
With rush and mushroom daisy chains
Hunting quietly towards Paddy Jack's bog
Like Mexican companeros dodging the Federalise.
I remember walking slowly back to the house
The butter spitting black on the pan
And the taste of mushrooms fried with salt.

Forgetfulness.

On becoming forty.

I left the lid off the teapot
Mid-stir and went
For a long walk in the woods
The hazel nuts are not near ripe
Back, there's a note from the milkman
For two week's milk unpaid,
My right shoe needs soled
The dog is to get his injections
I missed three dentists' appointments
I've run that run-over-cat fifty times
Going to meetings, dropping off the children
Trying to remember where we were going
Or what they were talking about,
People's names have been pushed back
Only "hello" will come into the mouth
and not "Michael"," Theresa"," Anne"
Your mother-loved sounds, I'm sorry.
Now each new blue day becomes grey
While ambition is turning to hope
Achievement to reminiscence
I can't hear the priest's sermon
For dreams of forever falling snow
Or flowers dancing in pollen hazed sunlight
It's September and I haven't been able
To get over March.

Saturday Night.

For My Mother.

A brown-paper parcel
Is slowly seeping blood
In corrugated rivulets,
Past quietly steeping peas
And tomorrow's peeled spuds
To the sink.

Small and freshly polished
Shoes sit winking in a row
Before the flames flicker.
The drying rack is at half mast
Its squealing pulleys stretched
With vests and stockings hanging empty.

On the backs of chairs
Sunday's clothes are ironed
With love in every crease
And all through the house
The laughter of shiny-faced children
And the smell of freshly boiling soup.

The Blackthorn Stick.

Clamped in a knarled knuckled fist

Is a twisted branch of fairy thorn,

With the malevolent power of De Dannan

Black and spiky, evil itself personified.

Solidly it holds steady his full weight

Unbending, like a third ebony leg.

At rest it exudes unearthly warnings

To fearless foes and faithless friends.

It has delivered manys a wicked stinging blow

Scudding across a trotting arse or

Held short, as a cudgel

On fair days and

Swung in a widening circle

Of smashing porter glasses.

Stars.

Pinhole stars sparkle
Through their dark screen,
A flowing vision cascading
From a long forgotten dream.

The scales on tiny fish
In shoals of a deep pool,
Darting through space
Thousands in their school.

Lovers Orion and Sirius
Together as legend said
Are settling now as spawn
Upon a gravely redd.

A Spell for You.

Twelve kisses on your brow each morning
Prepare you for the day
For all your pain
I'll give you flowers
And take each one away.
A single Foxglove blossom
Easeth self-consciousness,
Five Lavender stalks
To quell memory of past mistakes,
Cranesbills and Brides Blossom
Will mend a broken heart,
To all you're healing limbs
The yellow petals of St Johns Worts,
Eleven tiny forget Me Nots
And six clumps of Cuckooflower
Will ease feeling of loneliness,
A hedgerow shade of Violets
Inspires everywhere hopes of love
The Hawthorn's blossomed branch
Reassures those who've missed passions,
One Cornflower "blue bottle"
Dispels your heart's doubt
Catkins on your head, your joints and around your feet
Will free your secret dreams,
Lastly these four single cowslips for beauty
I'll plait into your hair
Evenly in an Elm-leaf pattern.
The sweet care of these flower-angels
Be around you forever
Seven times seven these wishes today I make for thee
Seven times happy
Seven times lucky
Seven times seven loved.

Swan's Down.

Two fluffs of down without quill are
On the oily-black bog bank bottom
High on the side of Carrickatuke's
Sidhe Fianna, now so long forgotten.

Where I was footing turf, yesterday's cut
Into long meandering wind-rows
When Lir came through tears to look,
And to lament weeping-full of sorrows.

I searched for Aoife and my beloveds
There on down below your cramps
Without trace among the mosses
Into the darkness with lit rush-lampthorns.

My eyes burned open with the darkness
A speckle was bog-cotton, was a sheep,
Was a star and not my loveliness.
Feet bog-dragged tired eyes without sleep.

Aed and Finola your mother's gift
My joys are gone forever without trace,
Con and Fiacra left as her parting life
I'll never more see your sweet faces.

My druids found this same swan's down
Far below by Lisletrims waters edge
And swore by spells you were undone
And turned to swans in a jealous rage.

But no need for you to heed this lore
For my children died in blood and gore,
Were slaughtered along that quiet shore
And were submerged that they be seen no more.

Shoes.

In memory of my Father.

Long ago when my world was under chairs
Quietly I watched the shoes.
My father's were black and shiny
One sole rested on the other's heel.

I held my breath and listened
He turned the pages of his newspaper,
The coals cracked in the fire
Smoke puffed out when the door opened.

In a big puff with a rustle of clothes
Came huge black patent shoes, the Canon,
Whispering like a housefly at a pane
And rubbing his hands together in loud rasps.

My granny's feet were tiny in blue lace ups
The steel tip of her umbrella threatening,
Granda swivelled his stick between two oxfords
Stopping the spin only when he was contradicted.

Friday callers wore yellow dealer boots
With elastic sides and cow-dung splatters
Talking of marts and cattle prices,
The conversation went round like a song,
Each person singing a lilting verse
With laughter as the chorus.

Rain Tomorrow.

This June day is slowly dying
The slipping sun says adieu
Silently as black wisps gather
The heralds of a dark tattoo.

All in rows the hawthorn bushes
Stand like first communion girls
Innocent they hide their blushes
Behind the blossoms of their veils.

Every flower of field and woodlands
Around their feet in garlands laid
Colours flare along the hedgerow
Fragrant in the evening shade.

Night bruises the rose-tinged hue
As the vixen barks her sorrows
Roosting birds relay the news
Alas there will be rain tomorrow.

Finian.

(Born 1995 - Died 1995)

When the blue dolphin schools
Clicked out your welcome to life,
In ultrasonic greetings
And leaping in spraying leaps
Heralded the summer's joy.
Then, Finian, you kicked,
Your first kicks in reply.
Sending leaving-cert books
Thudding to a lonely bedroom floor,
Where Fiannic tales of a swallowed moth
Would not explain your conception.
And when Gulf Stream waters broke
The dolphins turned south again,
Keening deeply in their booming tones.
Leaving you finally alone,
On golden Murreagh strand,
Seaweed braids in your lovely hair.

Awaiting an Old Friend.

Familiar hands now crossed and cold
Best suit with expressionless face,
No visible echoes of the man of old
Vanished as if never was without trace.

He will only live now in my nights,
I'll take you to matches and hunts again,
We'll be out all day and come home tight
After ceilidhing and thumbing home in the rain.

This is my final kiss of life to you
And the last we may feel together,
Laugh with me then, for its all we can do
And I'll wait on for you to visit forever.

Ashling Again.

Once upon and on and on
I visit you in your secret garden
You are lolling alone in the grass
Almost hidden in buttercup's gold
But not to me, not to me
You've saved those longing smiles for me
That book you're reading is held in three fingers
Your lips purse as you breathe haltingly
Exhaling in a stopping sigh,
You swish a blue cranefly away
With long elegant white fingers
Still seeming to beckon me towards you,
I'll pond-skate the sweat beads
On your brow, on your arms,
Your hair cascades to me
With the smell of May in flower
I move slowly over your body
Leaving a silver trail behind me,
If my antennae fronds sense your warmth
You show no realisation to me
If a moth-fluttering kiss falls on your lips
You are unaware of it
Your unknowing is my knowing
You haven't even seen me leave,
A cookoo-spit on the hem of your dress
Goodbye again for a few moments.

ONE SWALLOW.

Dog-rosehips were passionately their reddest,
Blackberries dangled everywhere unjustly black
And all along the nodding hedgerows sycamore trees
Were quietly closing their fists on the summer
When she finally conceded to herself to leave,
Joining the chattering throng that burdened the wires
Taking the news to Boyles, to Dalys, to Cullens.

Here, all summer long she had gathered love,
Midges under the canopies of Tullyglush's ashes,
Mayfly over the mirrored surface of Kavanagh's Lough
And moths by twilight all along the Callan's glen,
Alive again in this green place where she was born
Soaring and swirling her heart bursting with joy
Then, as now, she had no wish ever to leave.

Lastly there was just her and I, early,
Before cocks crow could waken men to judge
Slowly, under the morning sun her shadow passed
Across my face, slowly across my bare arms,
One final fleeting caress of momentary darkness,
Within that darkness I made a wish to stay;
As she alit now above me to whistle goodbyes.

Taking direction she south flew by Mullyash cairn
Over the broadening Fane and Cooley's plain of battles
In busy wing-beats over lonely Dermot and Grainne beds
Over Bruach Na Boinne, on and far on beyond the pale,
Turning seawards where Slaney-waters mingled with brine
Disappearing into the mists over Saint George's Channel.

Five Foxgloves.

On a high June hedge-bank five foxgloves flower,
Five fired Halloween skyrockets launched out
From wobbled jam-jars in violet comet trails
Leaving unnoticed on the bank Catherine wheels
Of bluebells, buttercups and tiny sparks of woodbine.

By July these five flowers are stooping full of fruit
Five nodding Lough Derg all night vigilers
Fighting to remain upright in the light of grace
And gently rocking in whispers to themselves
The five glorious mysteries on dangling rosary buds.

In August having spilt their seeds in its tens of thousands
They find it easier with their backs to the wall
To renounce the world, the flesh and the devil.
But even in the darkest nights of winter I won't recant
While purple remains the colour of kissed lips.

AUDIE MURPHY'S MEN

Scala Cinema Sunday Matinee.

He's shot this Sunday's last Apache
And now Audie's Palomino stallion rears up,
Its two front hooves kicking open the door
Just above the 'Push-Bar to Open' sign
Sending shafts of sunlight streaming in.

A gang of two hundred desperados burst forth
Following him through the streets of a border town
Shooting finger-colts wildly in the air
And reining in invisible horses menacingly
Turning Fletchers' corner-hooves skidding.

There's a stampede of longhorns in Cow Fair
And a fistfight outside Jack Short's saloon –
Probably half-breeds with too much firewater.
Scouts have spotted Apaches on the monument
Where they are surrounded and die a terrible death.
Their scalps will hang in Dalton Park, Crossmore Green
And Lir Gardens before sundown.

Audi has disappeared. We call after him,
He was last seen going up the Doctors Hill.
With a double swish of the reins
Heading for Mexico, we're sure.

THE MORRIGAN IN WINTER.

I'am in the autumn mists
that swirl among fallen leaves
on gravely paths,
in the trees whose
pointing skeletal fingers
the silver lattices hang,
almost invisibile,
in the dewy bobs that
bend each blade to earth,
where in my confusion
poisonous fungi grow.
I could choke your warm clouding breaths
in my coldest hoaring grips forever.
My final darkness comes
in a blanket of purest white
paralysing your soul
in its overwhelming void,
in my throes
I have killed your heroes
or shown your enemy
to their bloodied door.

Caroline's Morning.

To My Grandmother.

I see the black sequins on your hat
Glint in the morning's gold,
Marking your metronomic gait
As you walk to ten o'clock mass,
Climbing the hedgerowed lane
'Til you disappear from view.
A whispered voice comes
Across the fields carried by an angel,
It's you saying the blue rosary.
You'll call in to Norah's on your way home
She was good to her mother,
And over clattering cups
Swap news and knitting patterns.
At eleven your boney floured fingers
Will reverently knead the beads
While you wait for the cross
To rise on the wheaten.
The table is set with
Willow pattern cups upturned
And you pray quietly to yourself
As the angelus bell rings.

The Auction.

"On the instructions of the executors"
all fingered through
handled and examined
in lots of a pre-sale day for curiosity.
These most valued possessions,
A lifetime of gatherings,
His own kingdom of comfort
Where once he settled so easy.

A note from his long dead mother
In the pages of a book about Monaghan,

"Michael,
If you're this length over Christmas
Please stay a night. I have your bed made up for you.
I know you're busy in the parish, but I'd love to see you.
Love Mam x"

Now unvalued.

I browse with some shame through this life.
An intellect of books and letters
Good taste in furniture,
Remembrances in glass for good deeds
Committee days spent numberless.

All our letters
Become dusty bookmarks
Our books sit in dusty bookshelves
In our own furniture
In someone else's house.

The Clock.

Old friend,
Your lacquered silhouette fell
Across cradles and coffins.
You stood quietly
In the background,
Of first communion photos
And family gatherings.
I played on earthen floors
Accompanied by your
Reassuring "tick-tock"
Seemingly eternal.
On tippy-toes I peeped
Making fish-eyes, swaying
In your dented brass pendulum.
Chimes called us to the table
On frosty Sundays
Or sent us to school
On warm summer mornings.
You have been our guardian,
A witness to our passing
And still you greet us
With the whispering comfort
Of your regular pulse.

Thistledown Thoughts

No more pleasant thoughts
Visit my mind,
Than these thoughts of you,
So freely falling down.

Freed from your white opened palms
And floating like thistledown to me,
Little white lucent messages
Only I can almost see.

Falling on my mind, my heart,
And bouncing in downy kisses on my skin,
Kisses I send back to you
Mouthed in whispers on the breeze.

Sweeter than the bluebells of spring
Are the flowers which bloom at summers end,
Sorrel petals red are your lips,
Queen of the Field blossom your skin.

The No Divorce Court.

In sideways glances you have accused me

Forming depositions in your mind

Presented in chambers by changes of tone,

By derision, by turning your back

Initial counseling with your family

Led to briefings of friends and neighbours

You packed the jury with your news.

Your evidence first served, turned heads at mass

And hand over mouth conversations at work

Clerk of the courts on every corner discussed the case

But I can sense defeat in the children's eyes

And their instructed neutrality to me.

On remand I spend longer time alone

With light labour and loss of privileges.

I long for the higher court of flying vases

Of back to mother and envelopes on the mat

But I maintain my right to silence.

Above the Sounds of Water.

The Black Path from Annvale Mill to Keady.

Beside the ruins of an old mill's despair,
In the darkness of its deepest races,
A silver slice of the moon was gliding where
I heard the lovely sounds of water.

Storming currents swirling beech leaves
Overflowing the seized lock gates
In a continuously breaking wave
Making the lovely sounds of water.

Old men along these frozen bank walls
Came mourning in a ghostly phalanx
Murmurs mingle with fleeting footfalls
Murmuring above the sounds of water.

After sweeping the scutch room's nooks
Buffer boys swept home under the stars
Loudly coughing blood into their linen pokes
Coughing out above the sounds of water.

A newborn launched into the churning foam
In crying squeals departs its forlorn mother
Their keening spirits release the deepest moan
Keening loudly above the sounds of water.

In there my mind and heart was floating
Swirling with the stars and dead leaves.
Overflowing noisily among forgotten memories
Above the lovely sounds of water.

RAYMOND

In Memory of Raymond McCreesh

I think Cuchullain was small like Raymond
Though you wouldn't like me to call you small
For when the light of heroes lit in you
You swelled, you changed, distorted
Your face and body all contorted
The noise of the battle ringing
Incessantly in your head
The clattering of shields and swords
The whining whiz of arrows in flocks
The roars and rattles of the gored
And the names of the fallen
Appearing before you in ghostly swirls
chalked on the blackboard of your mind
You would not refuse the challenge
To the waters edge of the lonely battle ground
You still stood there defiantly contorted
A single pillar to your spine
Before the hosts of the enemy
The photographers
The pourers over of news
The editorialists
The cameramen,
The government propagandists,
Still you painfully bound your crios to the stone
They called the three daughters of Calatan
To release you from your curse
Bik, Brownie and the Dark
Still you bound and bound knuckles bleeding
They called the geasa of your family
Of the geasa of the church your family
Of the geasa of hospitality of the Irish race
And still you bound and tightened
And finally in your death throes
They poisoned you to make you yield
That your mind would unravel
But you would not
You would not
Let your sword to the ground.

The Man in the Moon.

When you left Ireland you wrote back to me,

"The moon shines in my bedroom window at night",

And I never stopped thinking about that.

Then, at the end of your letter, you wrote,

"I'll be thinking about you always, x x"

And I never stopped wondered if

You really were thinking about me.

Then looking at the moon, I realised,

To me you were, by moonbeam, only

Twice the distance of the moon from me

When lying on your bed in its brightness.

It was me who streamed in silver shafts

Through your window, over the floor to the bed,

Who turned in and out through your hair,

Who shone over your skin's translucent relief

And lit that blueing moon-glow in your eyes,

And though I never wrote it or said it

I was thinking about you, always

The man in the moon.

THE COCKFIGHT 1994

For Edward III 1365 and Oliver Cromwell 1653
(Who both banned cockfighting in Ireland.)

My direction was by the holly bush and on past the white piers
Off the road and up the side of a guttery double-hedged lane
Leading to a haggard in the "The Grey-rock Fort of the Celts"
Tierney's here with three regimes to take on all comers.
Cocks, the breeding that's known for hundreds of years
Are gathered from their various billeting for the fray
In boxes and wire cages on the straw of open cattle-trailers.
There in the three baler-twined circles will be the battles
Overhanging hawthorn branches are in June's full bloom
A sign of approval from the Fir Bolg in red-tinged blossom
"Three to one for Tierney" shouts Tierney's man
Proudly showing two big handfuls of paper money.
The bets are placed, notes under the foot, toes in the ring.
The first two birds are tossed and arc, heels raised together
In a leathery flapping encounter beaks and spurs gouging,
Crowd cheering each feint, each strike, every fluttering shriek
Till the yellow-crimson-spurred-three-toed foot of Tierney's
Holds the bleeding-beak-feathered-head-opposer to the ground.
Breaking for some pitch and toss and a glass of whiskey
From the converted ice cream-alcohol carts between fights.
And three times thirteen we've enjoyed this fray of forced nature
'Till the evening air and the swarming midges urge us home.
The last ice-cream cart leaves the field along the double hedge
All the traps are loaded. Only the three muddy circles remain,
Trailer-tail drops of hay in one corner and feathers on the breeze,
Edward, Oliver, you would have had a hell of a day.

Ceaping A Heifer.

For Noel Gallagher.

Bulging blank jelly eyes
Pupils oscillating in fear,
As your big awkward head swings
To and fro at face height.
Jetting clouds of warm air
Exhaled with bronchial rattles.
Seeming to always know
Where you're not wanted to go,
But running at each feint
Like a clumsy corner-back
Hooves skidding on the tar
And blocked almost everyway
With tail wildly up
You break through again,
Splattering as you go
Lumbering back up the road,
Followed by a band of ceapers
Like apaches, with ash plant spears
Sweeping you forward
On a flowing string of curses.

THE RAINDANCER.

In Memory Of Sean McKenna (Senior). Newry.

Revolution by steady iron revolution the wheel

Battered drills into sprays of spuds and stones,

At the day end the field is empty, brown and flattened

Except for twisted, broken blanched and scattered stalks

Discarded like the bindings of an army of hostages.

We manhandle Hessian bags upright on to the trailer,

Now becoming cold and bluer than the Arran banners,

Until he comes from the corner of the field

Walking to us, checking the dig, we knew,

His boots sinking almost stopping in the clods

Bending his knees in rain-dancing circles

His waistcoat's red lining flapping open

In rhythmical side to side movements

Pocket-coins rattling with each sliding step.

JOURNEY.

Once and only once we went away
For all journeys were the same,
Into the west, the wet wet west.
The car was stacked to the roof-rack,
Loose clothes, blankets and children,
A frenzy of coming and going 'till departure.
Wide-eyed faces splashed with holy water
We waved good-bye to the empty house.
The black car was morning-sun hot
Serpenting through Cavan's watery rampars,
One of the wee boys vomited rushed cornflakes,
Jetting everywhere between clasped fingers,
We slid into a swearing, stopping, disgorgment,
Swiping splashed shoes on the long acre,
Taking air while the blanket piles were turned.
Mammy held the heavens in her hands,
She called the saints by their Christian names,
As she rattled out the five glorious mysteries
The back seat answered the prayer-ends in a drone
And "Pray for us" in the litany of the saints.
"Tower of Ivory" "Pray for us"
"House of Gold" "Pray for us"
"Arc of the Covenant" "Pray for us"
"Galway 148 miles" "Pray for us"
"Help of the Sick", "Pray for us
It was Leitrim where I vomited.

AFTER THE SNOW.

Once the sun's long fingers

Sign with broken branches

On your whitened palms

You understanding go

Undressing slowly at first

The newly verdant pastures

Leaving white relief's

Only in sundial shadows

Behind the hedge-rows,

Departing drifts shelter

Like piebald gypsy ponies

Leaving one by one,

While we're not looking.

Through The Mill.

For William Kirk M.P.

Our boys pulled purple-headed stalks
Daddy forked the tied retting bundles in the bog
The girls scutched it into golden brown ponytails
To be spun and hand-loomed by the clacking bobbins
Only the fine Damask lace was bleached then,
Mammy needle pointed it in blinding deftness.

The loom tax your first real invention
Since your necessity was not ours
And a battery of beetlers
At a penny a week your bounty

We won't forget,
You beat the boys
You worked the men all hours
You took advantage of the girls
You put us through the mill.

The Path.

At Tisméan

Behind where the shingle stones banked
Before the weathered dry-stone walls
All along there where yellow lichens
Were clinging to the sides of stale salty pools,
A parting in the grass wound its way
Sea breezes gusting its hoared tufts
By the grass, by the stones; the path.
Here is where loneliness lingers
And the gulls forlornly cry.
I have followed you here
From deep inside where you left me
My heart like a drowned corpse
Flashed only faintly white through the blue
In gagging gasps, still seeking knowledge,
Along each of these stones,
Until the path ended desolately
The cliff edge falling to the sea far below
And then the sea breeze's pursed lips
Whispered "the journey is the destination"
Then I knew it was the path
That all along I had sought.

Skimming Stones on the Callan.

May 2003

My noisy river you have incised yourself into me
And my eroded black-brown heartloam
Your March floods have overflowed to
Where coltsfoot and the wood anemone
Blossoms garland you in swards of profusion,
Here and there tiny violets and shy bluebells
Peep from your diamond-rippled shade
Sent from the underworld to celebrate Balor's month.

The rooks are arguing in high bankside rookeries
And in the bushes two blackbirds are fly-dancing
Beak-kissing in a dizzy love-break to nest-building,
Dandelions in the open have all gone to seed
Lú's dancing beams have finished their work
They are the daytime fullmoons everywhere
Each a full translucently perfect orb on a stalk
Held out as a single wish candle to blow-
Will Assagh and Mochua ever walk your banks again?

The king fisher flashes from bush to bush
These Celtic Monks called it Éiniasc and drew
Its royal jade plumes to represent Jesus the fisher
It disappears near the undercut bank in a halo ripple
Beside where King Niall and the knight was drowned
I skim a stone along the surface of Girvan's pool
Breaking the pattern of circles from the rising trout
Plip! Plip! from noise Plip! Plip! to silence
I've broken your secret mirrored surface to discover
You've let me cross the timeline for a split-second.

A Pub Under the Trees.

Hear conversations low rustles
While condensation runs the glass,
In the fire bough-swayed branches crack

Here all is warm and safe
Held in a moment of time
Away from people with people

Where tree-ringed seasons pass in a flash
And always under the canopy
The swallow swiftly fly.

Everywhere in the gravel car park
Sycamore helicopter blades are down
A half smiled reminder of past success.

There in dimly-lit pollen-hazed rooms
Plots are hatching like opening seeds
Promising new death.

If only a little.

If only a little sunlight shone
Dappling maybe through branches and leaves
Or an angled winter sun streaking the shoulder
Of a long dark-mossed forgotten bank.

If only a little sunlight shone
And maybe in early spring or
Even maybe in autumn rather than
Sun-soaked flower-fielded summer.

If only a little sunlight shone
And it almost insignificant maybe
Landing on a single green leaf
Say the first coltsfoot leaf of spring.

If only a little sunlight shone
And with enough sunlight only to open
One pale-yellow petaled delicate flower
That flower would be for you.

Notes.

READING THE TREES
Carnagh wood is on the Castleblaney to Keady road.

KEADY'S WATER WHEEL
Clea Lake one mile from Keady.

AUCTIONEERS FOUNTAIN PEN
Fasces are a bundle of sticks with an axe used as a symbol of power by Roman emperors. Conacre is the system of land letting where farmland is leased for a single season from the first of March to the first of November.

WINTERBOURNE
A winterbourne is a stream that only runs during the winter months and dries up in spring when the rainfall reduces.

WILD MUSHROOMS
Companeros are Mexican bandits and they are hunted by the Federalise, the Federal Government army.

THE BLACKTHORN STICK
De Dannan literally the people of the goddess Dana. The pre Celtic inhabitants of Ireland who were believed to have magical powers that were connected to Fairy Forts and especially the Hawthorn tree and blossom that grew there.

STARS
Orion and Sirius two large stars that were by Egyptian legend the first two Gods in the heavens and their offspring are all the other stars in the firmament. A redd is a pebbly upstream riverbed where salmon mate and lay their eggs.

A SPELL FOR YOU
The Flowers and cures in this poem are from Dr. Culpepers Herbal Remedies published in 1850. The remedies are that described for the symptoms. This book belonged to my great grand mother.

SWANS DOWN
Carrickatuke is the mountain between Keady and Newtownhamilton that overlooks Co. Monaghan and Lisletrim Lough where by legend the children of Lir were turned into swans. Sidhe Fianna was the name of Lir's fort that was by legend on Carrickatuke. Aobh was Lir's wife who died at the birth of the twins Con and Fiacre. Lir then married her sister Aoife who was a disciple of the god Alpus. Her jealousy of the children was so strong she finally decided to do away with them. Wind-rows are sods of turf on their ends in rows to dry in the wind.

FINIAN
Murreagh Strand is in county Clare and the nearest Chapel and graveyard is St. Finians. According to the stories of the Fianna Cuchullain was conceived when the sun god Cian landed in the form of a moth on his mothers Ethlinn's goblet and she drank it and became pregnant.

THE MORRIGAN IN WINTER
The Morrigan is an ancient Irish Goddess of war. She could take many forms and used spells and deception on her enemies. She fell in love with Cuchullain and was angered when he spurned her. Her most famous form is as the Raven on the shoulder of the dead Cuchullain.

RAYMOND
A Crios is a woven belt worn by warriors. The three daughters of Calatan put a curse on Cuchullain on the way to his final battle. The word geasa is a word from Irish which means obligation or duty, an innate sense of honour that you are impelled to do follow regardless of personal consequences.

THE COCKFIGHT
Tierney is allegedly a Tyrone breeder of fighting cocks. A regime is a series of thirteen fights usually a "stable" versus "stable" contest. Individual fights are important but to win a regime with your birds is the ultimate accolade. The Fir Bolg are pre Celt inhabitants if Ireland also known as De Dannan. Pitch and toss is an old street game played with two pennies and bets are placed on heading or tailing both coins.

CEAPING A HEIFER
To Ceap is to block, chase or cut off or catch. It is a transition word from the Irish and is still often used today in the country.

THE RAINDANCER
Arran Banners is a variety of potato.

THROUGH THE MILL
Retting is part of the process of making linen. The pulled flax is tied in bundles and soaked or "retted" in a bog hole to soften the outer husk before being scotched to remove the husk leaving the hair like flax strands. Damask lace was the highest quality hand made linen lace similar to "Carricmacross Lace".

SKIMMING STONES ON THE CALLAN
The River Callán in Irish means noisy.
Balor is the underworld Celtic god.
The month of May in Irish "Beáltaine" is named after him.
Lú is the son of the Celtic Sun god.
Assagh and Mochua were contemporises of St. Patrick who founded Monasteries in the Callan valley and surrounding hills.
King Niall King of all Ireland was drowned in the river 840 A.D. aged 55
Éiniasc is the "fishing bird" in Irish or kingfisher.